PROCEEDINGS

OF THE

CONGRESS OF THE PEOPLE'S LEAGUE

OF THE

OLD AND NEW WORLD.

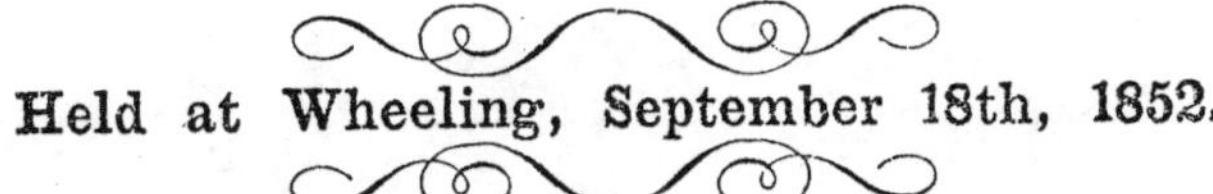

Held at Wheeling, September 18th, 1852.

PHILADELPHIA:
A. KETTERLINUS, *Printer*, N. E. cor. of Third & Race Streets.
1852.

PROCEEDINGS.

A preparatory meeting came to order by the election of Dr. K. Homburg, of Indianapolis, as Provisional Chairman, and of E. Schlæger, of Boston, as Secretary. The following sixteen delegates, from thirteen Unions, presented their credentials.

L. KIRCHNER, of Troy, N. Y.
Dr. K. HOMBURG, of Indianapolis, Ind.
G. MUELLER, of Cleveland, Ohio.
R. FISHER, S. STROBEL, Prof. J. N. WINKLE, } of Wheeling, Va.
G. BACZKO, of Albany, N. Y.
A. GERWIG, of Cincinnati, O.
C. GOEPP, W. ROSENTHAL, } of Philadelphia, Pa.
J. ROTH, C. HOFFMAN, } of Pittsburgh, Pa.
L. MEYER, of Boston, Mass.
E. SCHLÆGER, for Roxbury, Charlestown and Webster, Mass.
W. ROTHACKER, for London, England.

The Deputy of the Executive Board submitted the report of the past history of the League (see Appendix A.), and the propositions of the Board in relation to the action of Congress, which were referred to a business Committee; and the Financial Report, which was also referred (App. B.).

FIRST REGULAR SESSION.

City Hall, Sept. 20th.

The following permanent officers were elected:

President, DR. HOMBURG.

Vice Presidents, R. FISCHER and L. ROOS.

Secretaries, E. SCHLÆGER, J. N. WINKLE and C. HOFFMANN.

Letters were read from John Ross, Brighton, Mass., from the Revolutionary Union of Reading, Pa., from the Union of Richmond, Va., from A. Goegg, London, from L. Kossuth (App. C.), and from the Central European Committee (App. D.).

Standing Committees were appointed, No. 1., on American politics; No. 2, on European affairs; No. 3, on National Loans; No. 4, on Military Organizations; No. 5, on Organization and Agitation; No. 6, on Publications.

Evening Session.

Committee No. 1, reported a series of Resolutions on the leading objects of the League (Appendix E.), which were adopted and referred back to the Committee, with instructions to report an Address to the American People, founded upon them (see Address to the American People.).

Also a supplementary report, in relation to the present position of American parties (App. F.), which was adopted.

Sept. 21ts. Morning Session.

The report of Committee No. 2 was submitted and adopted, and referred back to the Committee, with instructions to expand it into an Address to the European Democracy (App. G.).

The report of Committee No. 3, (App. H.) was adopted.

The report of Committee No. 4, (App. I.) was adopted.

Afternoon Session.

The Committee on Organization submitted a series of propositions, which resulted in the following resolutions:

1st. To amend Sect. I. of the Constitution so as to read: The name of this Organization shall be, "*The People's League of the Old and New World.*"

2. The political Committee shall consist of ten members and three substitutes (Const. Sec. VI. E.).

3. The Executive Board (Const. VI. A. b.) shall consist of three members and three substitutes.

4. To strike out as superfluous the paragraph of the constitution providing that the Congress shall decide by a simple majority on the competency of every delegate.

Evening Session.

The following organic resolutions were adopted:

The Executive Board is to be located at Boston, and shall appoint the time of meeting of the next Congress, to be held at Cleveland, Ohio.

Members of the Political Commission: Amandus Goegg, Chas. Goepp and Arnold Ruge. Substitutes: F. Siegel, J. Ronge and Loewe of Calbe.

Members of the Board: P. Wagner, E. Schlaeger, L. Meyer. Substitutes: W. Wesselhoeft, H. C. Ahlborn, B. Domschke.

The following means of agitation were enjoined:

1st. The Branch Unions are to furnish the board with monthly reports, through their corresponding secretaries.

2nd. To concentrate and absorb all the progressive elements in their locality.

3rd. The board is to issue a circular to all the offices of all the newspapers in the Union, requesting them to insert the official documents of the League, and articles upon the objects of the League, as well as to aid the cause editorially.

4th. The Branch Unions are called upon to encourage their members to further the cause by means of the press, wherever attainable and, if not publishable otherwise, to transmit them to the Board for insertion.

Resolved to publish the Address to the American People in the English and German languages, in an edition of 2000 copies.

Also to publish the Address to the European Democracy in 10,000 German, 5,000 English, 5,000 French and 5,000 Italian copies.

And to publish the Proceedings of Congress in 2,000 copies.

Dr. Gerwig placed one third of the proceeds of the publication of his work on "Caspar Hauser," at the disposal of the League, and requested their exertions in aid of its circulation.

Thanks were voted to the outgoing board and to Amandus Goegg, for their exertions in agitation.

Congress then adjourned *sine die.*

K. HOMBURG, *President.*

E. SCHLAEGER, *Secretary.*

(APPENDIX A.)

Report of the Executive Board of the American Revolutionary League.

In September, 1851, Gottfried Kinkel came to Philadelphia, to raise funds for the expenses incurred by the German Revolutionists in their efforts to rid that country of the yoke of its despots. The plan he had adopted was an imitation of the Italian National Loan, so successfully negotiated by Mazzini. The German fugitives were at that time torn by violent dissensions, in which Kinkel was implicated, and thereby the confidence in his undertaking considerably impaired. To overcome this obstacle, Kinkel proposed to leave all the moneys collected, in the hands of a committee to be appointed at Philadelphia, there to remain until these dissensions should be ended, and a harmonious organization of the fugitive democracy perfected.—The committee at the same time, addressed the leaders of the contending factions, residing in London, exhorting them to harmony. Kinkel, however, finding the public mind at Baltimore and other places more favorable to him, succeeded in inducing the committees appointed at those places, to send their moneys to Europe, as soon as collected.—The Philadelphia Committee thus found itself read out of the line. The replies of the Londoners, also, were such as to make a union of the two parties more improbable than ever.

In this emergency the committee resolved to devolve the mannagement of the affairs of the party upon a Congress of the "German American Democracy, favorably disposed to the European Revolution." This Congress assembled at Philadelphia, on the 29th of January last, and established the 'American Revolutionary League for Europe,' the constitution of which was published in the Tribune and Public Ledger. Its declared object was cooperation in the veritable liberation of the European continent, by means of collections of moneys, military drill and exercise, and agitation. An executive committee was appointed to serve until the meeting of the next Congress, at Wheeling, on the 18th of September.

A leading member of the Congress was Amandus Goegg, who had been prominent in the Baden revolution of '49, and had left London on purpose to attend its sittings. After the adjournment he turned his attention to the extension of the League, and succeeded in establishing auxiliary unions in fifty of the principal towns of the free States of the Union. On his return from the West, at Buffalo, he crossed the path of Kossuth, who then began to understand the importance of the Germans in these movements, and formally recognized the League. Subsequently, at Boston, he even declared himself a member of it, and reiterated this declaration at New York, in the memorable words "To this League I entrust the culture of the tender blade which I have planted; may they screen it from the blast of winter, and make it sprout into the tree of Freedom."

Goegg and Kossuth returned to England together; the former has established a branch league in that country, which bids fair, in many respects, to equal its cis-atlantic prototype. It is for the congress at Wheeling, and those whom it represents to carry on the work so well begun.

APPENDIX B.

Report of the Finance Committee.

The fund of the American Revolutionary League consists of the following items : —

RECEIPTS.

1st.	The proceeds of a fair held at Philadelphia, by the Philadelphia Committee, for the revolutionary fund,	$ 272 00
2nd.	German National Loan,	249 50
3rd.	Contributions from Branch Associations,	36 26
	Whole amount,	$ 556 76

EXPENDITURES,

Incurred according to the report of the treasurer, dated the 14th Spt., 1852.	$ 310 69
Balance,	$ 246 07
The claim of $ 40 against Mr. Fickler included, gives an amount of	$ 286 07

remaining in the treasury.

Signed, HENRY TIEDEMANN, M. D., *Treasurer.*

Approved by the Committee.

G. BACZKO, *Chairman.*

APPENDIX C.

LETTER FROM KOSSUTH

To the Congress of the American Revolutionary League for Europe.

The warm fraternal sympathies, extended to my efforts by the German citizens of America at every stage of my journey through the States, have become an additional tie to bind me to the cause of German liberty, which I have ever considered as intimately allied, or rather identical, with that of the liberation of Hungary and Itály. The brotherhood of these nations is not only the result of their common thirst for freedom, but is a requirement of the actual state of affairs, and a logical deduction from the significance of passing events. Not that the special alliance of these nations is to be considered as an exclusion of others, not as if it were intended to assert the all-sufficiency of these three nations, or their right to reject the hand of friendship, wherever offered; whoever is enlisted in the common cause of the delivery of the continent from the shackles of despotism, by means of the fraternity of the peoples, needs no further recommendation as a welcome ally.—But while some nations are prevented, by the nature of things, from entering into the front line of battle, another nation has been so favored by circumstances, that in its very breast, the hydra of absolutism with all its horrors, may be annihilated at a blow. A few short days, perhaps hours, will suffice to revolutionize the fortunes of France, without the necessity of a tedious war against oppression; France once awakened from the iron embrace of the torpor, which now seems to overwhelm her, the electric stroke of freedom will once more tingle through all the nations of Europe. But Germany, Hungary and Italy cannot achieve their liberties at a blow; with them it is the price, not of a brief revolution, but of a lengthy struggle, and the foe they have to combat is ever the same, the perjured, bloodstained dynasty of Austria, whose yoke extends from Hamburg to the Faro, and from the Rhine to the Rothturm Pass; thwarting every effort of revolt. While this power exists, neither Germany, Hungary nor Italy can be free; the liberty of every one of the three is dependent upon that of the other two, and their common liberation alone affords a guarantee of duration and security. The common foe, the necessity of concert, the certainty of failure in case of isolation, are the base upon which this confederation is reared, and which entirely identifies their efforts at revolution.

From this point of view I am enabled to point out to you many stars of hope in the dark night of doubt and dread, even tho' much of what might be told must still be withheld from publicity.—American travelers, one of your German fellow-citizens among them, confirm the statement, that the people are prepared at a moment's notice, to rise in a body against their oppressors; no reserve was maintained in intercourse with Americans, and every one spoke freely of the prospects of the coming contest. Italy is fully organized, and awaits the signal; it is no longer a secret conspiracy that is at work, but a universal resolve of the nation, everywhere manifested, and hardly to be longer restrained In Germany the idea of the republic and of the necessity of a combination is daily gaining ground, which is all the more encouraging, the more the past developments of that country impede its harmonious organization; while in the East, Russia is preparing a crisis in the Turkish empire, and meditating an almost immediate occupation, thus verifying, to my own astonishment, the prediction uttered by me at Buffalo and Syracuse, and placing into the nearest future those developments, which must necessarely precede and advance the liberation of the nations. Wherever we cast our eyes the conviction obtrudes itself, that the hour for action is at hand, and that it is time for the friends of Europe in America to enter on the task which devolves upon them.

If I understand aright the position of the Revolutionary League now represented at Wheeling, it has an internal and an external bearing. In regard to the former, I hope that the Germans in America, aware that they hold the balance of power in their hands, have not thrown their talent unconditionally into the scale, without having first, in conformity with the platform of Philadelphia, received from the man of their choice an assurance of the assertion of such principles, as shall further the liberty of Europe, and rescue the honor and the interest of America. If this has not yet taken place, it will only become me to remind you, that the nearer the approach of the decisive moment, the more important will be the maintenance of an independent position, and that if you should be induced by the sound of a party name to compromise your influence in advance, it may be long before the time will recur, which shall give the German citizens of America a weight in the scale such as they can now possess.

In regard to the external relations of the league, it is necessary in the first place to *furnish the means of action*, and secondly to *choose the proper men to apply them*. The want of material aid becomes more pressing, the nearer the hour of battle approaches. These means are expressed in a single word, their name is *money*. With a sufficiency of means it is easy to influence the fates of Europe, while with inadequate means, the greatest activity is able to attain but partial results, which for that very reason, subsequently call for far greater sacrifices, than would have been needed for a powerful effort at the proper time. Relying upon the sympathy of the Germans in America, who have so nobly and actively sustained the Hungarian cause, I have, on leaving the United States, entrusted the General Agency of the Hungarian Loan to the German Committee in Philadelphia; and the instructions of my friend, Dr. Tiedeman, which he is authorized to communciate to you in so far as they refer to this subject, will show that I have not by any means intended to monopolize for my native country the proceeds of the loan, but am prepared, in the spirit of fraternity and of the confederation of the three nations, to place a portion of the funds at the disposal of the Revolutionary League, for the special purpose of the liberation of Germany.

It is far easier to extend and turn to account a movement already commenced, than to originate a new one. The mere practical preparations for a new financial project would unavoidably delay it beyond the time for which it could be useful. I cannot but say, therefore, that it is my firm persuasion that more could be achieved even for the special liberation of Germany, by an energetic and official emission of the Hungarian Bonds on the part of the League, than by any new project which could be devised. This enterprise is also more likely to succeed than any other among that portion of the citizens of America, who are not of immediate German descent, the more so as it embraces the best chances of an ultimate reimbursement of immediate pecuniary sacrifices; for, however the opinions of individuals may differ upon the final issue of the European struggles, all are agreed that a conflict is not to be avoided, and that from the moment of its breaking out, the Hungarian bonds, already known and circulated, will receive a value "on'change," which will enable any one who is prevented from awaiting the ultimate decision, to receive a value for his bonds.

If these views should have the good fortune to meet with your concurrence, my request is to pass resolutions to this effect, and to set the organs of the League to work for their execution. But even if it should be otherwise, I still hope you will not forget that the destinies of my country are identified with those of Germany, and that you will prove to the world, with the consistency so peculiar to the German character, that the seed I have sown in America, and consigned to the tender care of the Germans, has not been lost by my unavoidable absence, but has continued, on the contrary, to flourish under your care.

In regard to the choice of men proper for the application of the means to be collected, I have repeatedly given it as my opinion, that the greater the difficulty of a rational concentration of the multifarious products of German history in a single individual, the greater is the propriety of the direction of the movement by *the great collective body* of the German citizens of America. But the authority for this control will be strong or feeble in proportion to the amount of means furnished by them. But even when these means are supplied, it will be necessary that the organs of their disbursement should be near the principal theatre of action. They must reside in Europe. The state of affairs is such that I must be permitted earnestly to commend this circumstance, as well as the importance of such an election, to your careful deliberation. Should the League decide to make choice of a committee, consisting of a limited number, perhaps of not more than three German patriots,—selecting one from the North, and one from the South of Germany, and one acquainted, from personal experience, with American men and manners,—and should they conclude to fill the latter place by the person of one, who enjoys the confidence of a large portion of Germany, and whose present retirement is assuredly designed to be but temporary, and only to endure until he shall be enabled to return with renewed vigor to his station,—in that case I hope he will consent to exchange his retirement for the post of danger.

As regards myself, well knowing that a stranger is only so far privileged to interfere in the affairs of a nation not his own, as the fraternity of nations and the identity of purposes will warrant, —rest assured that, whoever may be the object of your choice, I shall ever be ready to labor with him hand in hand.

May the spirit of concord direct your proceedings, and may you, by the blessing of God, enjoy the proud consciousness of having achieved for the republican principle represented by the United States, an adequate position among the powers of the earth, of having rescued from decay the glorious future of your adopted country, and of having earned for the Germans of America, the high honor of the regeneration of European liberty.

L. KOSSUTH.

London, August 31. 1852.

APPENDIX D.

Central European Democratic Committee,
LONDON, August 26, 1850.

CITIZENS: —You have learned, that the Republic, if not an empty sound,—is a standard, the oriflamme of a humanitary faith; —that democracy is a principle for which there is no local, but only a universal triumph, a principle which knows neither an Old World nor a New. The World is its sphere, the human family is its aim; the association of all, its tactics.

You have heard the arguments which combat the Holy Alliance of privilege and of despotism with the alliance of equality and liberty; you have been mindful of the teachings of the past, and have not forgotten that men of France hastened to set the seal of solidarity upon the first struggles of the American revolution. You have listened to the still small voice within, appealing to the unity of the human soul in thought and action. And you have set yourselves to the task of realizing in Europe the faith you profess in the United States of the West.

In the name of the European Democracy, we salute your action as a brilliant token of the fraternal vocation of the human race, and as an augury of the triumph of its holy cause.

The Democracy of Europe counts upon you.

We count upon your assistance at the first outbreak of the struggle for which we are preparing, and which we hold to be more nearly impending than you may be prepared to believe. The first days of the struggle are decisive of its issue; it is for them that a concentration of power is necessary.

Haste to extend the organization of your League.—Let all men of soul and purpose fly to the standard you have so nobly upraised. In view of the imminence of the crusade, let a feeling of harmony and of action efface all individual differences. Labor seriously, unitedly, as if you had an eternity before you. Collect henceforth, and transmit with the least possible delay to your European brethren, all the material practical aid you can, bending to your toil as if from day to day the battle might commence: Such is now your mission; its accomplishment will assure you the gratitude and the love of the European Democracy.

For the Central European Committee.

LEDRU ROLLIN,
JOSEPH MAZZINI,
D. BRATIANO,
ARNOLD RUGE.

APPENDIX E.

RESOLUTIONS.

1. In consideration of the misery of Europe and the power of America, in remembrance of the disease of the old world, and the healthful and promising growth of the new; in view of the despair of the subjects from whom we are descended, and of the energy of the freemen to whom we belong, we call upon our American fellow citizens to remember that the hopes of Europe have placed their stay upon America.

2. We have no cause of complaint against the American people for their resolution to reserve their sympathies for the fulfilment of their own peculiar mission; that mission being comprehensive enough for the powers of any people. We do not ask America to transcend the task history has assigned her, but we are entitled to ask that she should comprehend her whole task, and enter upon its execution.

3. The American Union grew out of the wants of independent, enterprising, freedom-loving States. The thirteen States were suffering for want of an uninterrupted internal trade, a common regulation of commercial affairs, united post office, the mutual extradition of criminals and recognition of matters of record, and a mutual guaranty of republican institutions against external and internal foes.

4. These grievances were removed, under the motto, "*E pluribus unum.*" A multiplicity of States was recognized as a relic of barbarism, which must yield to the truth that where governments have a unity of object, there can be but *one* government as a means to obtain them. "E pluribus unum," in its most extended sense, is the watchword of the American Union.

5. In the acquisition of Louisiana, the Father of American democracy, the Declarer of Independence, Thomas Jefferson, unconsciously perhaps, but none the less irrevocably, set his seal upon the maxim. The annexation of Texas and California was equally inevitable. Cuba and Canada are destined to follow their

example. Even the Islands of the Pacific, in the awakening dawn of their political life, manifest the same attraction towards the focus of the nineteenth century.

6. America is now more intricately connected with the people of Europe, than were the Thirteen States with each other, at the memorable epoch of '87. The lightning is not yet the bearer of despatches between them; but already the postal communications are incredible in numbers. The emigration of a few years will exceed the population of the States at the formation of the Union. There is scarce a family in the German portions of Europe, the members of which are not severed by the waves of the Atlantic. The impediments of commerce are more embarassing, the impunity of criminals more dangerous, the conflict of the copy and patent laws more iniquitous, the severance of judical records more onerous, the absence of a mutual guaranty of republican freedom more hurtful and more ignominous to both parties, than it ever was between the disunited republics of America.

7. For the security of American liberty we demand the liberation of our sister nations of Europe; for the fostering of American prosperity we ask the disenthralment of European trade and manufactures; for the preservation of the American Union we demand its extension over the states of Europe, the extension of the American principle of "E pluribus Unum" over the European world, which is hopelessly sinking from the absence of its introduction.

8. The spread of American liberty, even by force of arms, is not a conquest but a liberation; for as the principles of our government is self, or rather non-government, its extension involves not the introduction, but the abrogation of force and violence.

9. As Italy cleaves the Mediterranean, so does America divide the Oceans. As Rome looked forth upon her orbis terrarum, so America casts her eyes around the shores of the Ocean world. The universal Empire of the future is her portion. The empire not of conquest and subjection, not of tradition and death, not of national rivalry and clannish hate, but of fraternity, equality and freedom.

May her destiny be speedily fulfilled.

APPENDIX F.

Position of the League with regard to American Parties.

The "People's League of the Old World and the New" has, in its statutes, chosen not Europe alone, but especially America, for the field of its labors. To give this agitation in America a practical bearing, it will be necessary to be guided in the adoption of measures by reference to American men and things. Foremost among these considerations are the positions, principles, and measures of the political parties now contending for the occupancy of the influential executive and legislative offices of the government; the issue of the contest will exert an undeniable influence upon the attitude assumed by this Republic towards the rest of the civilized world.

The practibility of uniting the activity of the League into a common stream with the various drifting elements of progress, so as to give a converging direction to their efforts, was the subject of mature deliberation by the present Congress.

These deliberations have resulted in the conviction that to recommend the support of one of the existing parties, equally uncommitted as they are, upon the policy we advocate, would be an unwarrantable dictation to the individuals friendly to the cause. We prefer to recommend a line of action which, without interfering with votes and candidates, has for its object the attainment of a general unity of purpose, from which a unity of execution may be expected to follow, not by the devices of electioneering advocacy, but by the irresistible force of logical necessity. These views are expressed in the following resolutions:

1. The People's League, as such, enters the service of none of the existing political parties, nor does it assume to act as a party of its own.

2. The People's League will endeavor to bring about a harmonious action of the various elements of progress, and to strengthen their influence, by cultivating the political intelligence and independence of the citizen, by advocating the great object of the League, and by encouraging every rational and timely progressive movement.

3. It is the especial duty of the branch unions of the League, and of the heads of their respective organizations, to agitate the questions arising out of our common purpose, the unceasing spread of American liberty among all who stand in need of freedom, and to impress them upon the hearts and minds of the people.

4. The application of the convictions thus matured to the course proper to be taken in reference to the impending elections, is left to the unrestrained judgment of the individual citizen.

APPENDIX G.

The People's League of the Old and New World, to the European Democracy.

Standing on the confines of two periods of history, where the effete ingredients of the one are undergoing a reoslution into their original elements, while the other as yet casts the shadow of its coming events but dimly before; called upon to harmonize opposite tendencies, and organize multifarious elements; the American Revolutionary League for Europe found in the absence of a central, comprehensive, but unitary idea, an insuperable obstacle to the fulfilment of the hopes so well warranted by the noble and apparently well-timed character of its purposes.

The position of the League is beset with difficulties.

We are to strengthen and extend our organization, without exciting the distrust or jealousy of other political combinations. We are called upon at once to seek especially the favor of the Germans, and to avoid giving cause of offence to other nationalities. We are to direct American politics to external affairs, without furnishing the spirit of exclusiveness with color for the insinuation, that we are laboring to establish a foreign party. We are to give the European republicans aid and counsel, and yet to eschew the semblance of forwardness.

To bring the dormant powers of the League to bear upon the condition of the world, it was necessary to restore harmony into this conflict of duties, to resolve these inferior opposites into the unity of a higher, a universal idea.

The tide of nations pouring incessantly into the countries West of the Atlantic, the American pilgrimage of the great spokesman of down-trodden Europe, and the force with which he urged the world-wide importance of America upon the coming struggle for life and death, the preference of the industrial classes of England for American forms of government with their freedom of personal and intellectual intercourse, all point to a transfer of the central gravitation of society to the republic of the United States, all evince the incapacity of the European body politic to initiate the solution of the great problems of the time.

But hitherto it has been found impossible to apply the vast motive power of the young republic to this initiation of the world's reform.

In vain have the bleeding wounds of Europe been opened to coerce the sympathies of the United States into the channel of their relief; in vain has the mighty voice of the age poured forth its wondrous tones to obtain admission for the principle of intervention for non-intervention into the cycle of leading American aspirations.

An individual may be induced to bestow his charity upon the suppliant whose maims and moans offend the eye and ear, but a nation obeys the voice of a necessity higher than the promptings of a momentary impulse, its heart can never so far overcome its calm reflection, as to allow pity for the sufferings of another nation to force it from the strongly marked course of its own historical development.

The ideas of sympathy, of intervention, of duties between nation and nation on simply moral grounds, belong to a subordinate sphere of the human mind, to the sphere of the affections; they are not inscribed upon that code which, like the fate of ancient time, dictates irrevocably the walk of nations. They have no right to be heard beside the just demands of historical destiny.

The history of a nation which at a given epoch appears as the custodian of the fortunes of humanity, regards as sovereign only the well founded interest of the nation resulting from the spirit of its people, just as the individual man, in the highest stage of cultivation, in all the so-called good and virtuous actions of his life, pursues the same aims as in those usually ascribed to meaner motives, the perfection and realization of his refined and ennobled individuality.

It was necessary to evolve a new idea, which, instead of aiming to enlist the more active sympathies of America in the ranks of the revolutionary forces of Europe, under the watchword of morality and abstract right, is calculated at once to express and exhaust the highest interests of American nationality, and to infuse into the inextricable complication of the revolutionary aims and interests of Europe, the light of a grand and simple clearness and consistency.

It is the idea of the annexation of the now revolutionary world to the Union of the American States, which furnishes a central point for the diverging threads of European efforts, it is in the extension of American republicanism over the political world, that we find the expression of the necessity commanded by the destinies of the people's, and the guaranty of their welfare.

As, before the iron tread of the Roman legions, the mightiest nations, surrendering their peculiarities to the assimilating power of the Eternal City, were absorbed into its universal empire, so, by looking into the seeds of time, we find America destined *"to resolve the multiform national elements of Europe into the universal spirit of true Americanism."*

As the faint swelling of the sea at the first breath of the rising wind, denotes the direction of the storm, so the past annexations, which led to the entrance of Texas and California into the confederacy, point to the mightier powers soon to be put forth by the young republic, in the performance of her tremendous task.

Cuba and Canada, as well as Mexico, will be the next trophies of the instinctive energies of America. Having thus traversed the whole length and breadth of the Northern Continent, the young Giant of the West will cast his eyes upon the ancient East, the cradle of his existence, and stretch his eager arms across the sea, to repay the debt of civilization, which arose in Asia, by revivifying those mouldering empires with the advent of the long lost child of the skies, the ever worshipped genius of liberty. Do not even the islands of the Pacific, attached to us by means of California, in obedience to a law of political gravitation, steer their course towards the focus of the world, the broad skirted mistress of the Oceans, America? The civilized world has attained that stage of cultivation, in which a community of interests requires a common form of administration.

The increase and complexity of commercial arrangements, the facilities of intercommunication, between Europe and America, call for unitary commercial laws, for common coinage, weights and measures, for a single post office, for a mutual guaranty of republican institutions,—with a voice of peremptory necessity, before which the disputes of European politicians on the contest of class interests, on the question of centralization or decentralization, sink into insignifiance.

Colossal as may at first appear this idea of the United States of the Civilized World, to be formed by crystallization around the nucleus now existing in America, the experience of seventy-six years in which this political formation has perpetuated and extended itself over an immense extent of territory, conclusively proves its adaptability to an area of any size. The nations composing the civilized world are now in a position analogous to that of the thirteen States that formed this union, in 1787. The necessity of a common regulation of common interests then impelled these thirteen States to establish a more perfect union, of the expediency of which the present prosperity of the republic is a token. The past of America is a sketch of the greater picture of the World Republic, of which her oceanic position qualifies her to become the mistress, as the position of ancient Italy in the middle of the Mediterranean, assigned to it the hegemony of the lands skirting that inland sea.

If the problem of our age, to produce man in his perfection by means of the greatest external and internal welfare, is to be solved, if the word "Man" is inscribed upon the portal of the future, the assimilation of the elements of ancient nationalism is only to be accomplished in the United States: for only in that nation, which is not a nation, but, in the true sense of the word, a people, the narrowness of its component parts is made to yield to the higher unity of Americanism. Louisiana with its heterogeneous French traditions, California with its collapsed Spanish life and manners, demonstrate the irresistible absorption of the partialism of the old nationalities, into the universality of Americanism. In Europe we look in vain for a power capable of originating this World's Reform, this establishment of a common commercial legislation, of a general World's Union of Sovereign and Independent States.

There is a certain hopelessness, a flitting uncertainty of design, in the action of the revolutionary politicians. They know not what to do. In a revamp of the revolutions of the past they feebly hope to find that lasting amelioration which is only to be obtained by participation in a league, which has tested and approved the all-controling principle of self-government, of the absolute sovereignty of the individual, and carried the principle of a Union of Sovereign States to the degree of perfection it has obtained in America. The factitious conflicts of national interests, aggravated into social evils, by long duration and suicidal cultivation admit of no correction not attended and facilitated by the drain of overflowing elements, and the opportunities of expansion afforded by the intense industrial vitality of the Republic of the West.

The unrestricted intercourse of nations, regulating, by common consent, their commercial relations, is the indispensable negative pre-requisite of any solution of the social problem. It is only in the federal union of the civilized world, gathered around the Romans of modern time, that that equalization of individual welfare is attainable, which forms the pursuit and the riddle of our Sphinx-like times.

The immense resources of America will afford the stores for the world's citadel, by which the starving garrison will obtain the respite necessary to the acquisition of a higher grade of mental and moral culture, without which social equality will ever be but the evanescent creature of an hour.

Russia is the back-bone of European despotism. America is destined to become a second Russia, the Russia of freedom, whose powers will be as far superior, as the onset of a people conscious of its purpose overbears the ranks of hirelings fighting battles not their own.

To bring America to the perfect understanding of this mission is what we conceive to be the task assigned to us, and to all true revolutionaries in Europe and America. The various parties of the champions of freedom, who have been scattered far and wide, in search of the spell by which to burst the rock of the future, will find in the idea of the "Union of the World around the States of America," the centre and the practicable basis on which the aspirations of errant politicians may be introduced to the tangible realities of the present.

Democrats of Europe! It is for you to secure the services of this American rearguard in the battles of European liberty, by removing the petty differences of nationalities, the polypolitical relics of barbarity and ignorance.

The result of a patient experimental test of the policy of the American states is before you, the unexampled growth of their territory, power, prosperity, and civilization, points to this form of government as satisfying the requirements of the present stage of human development.

The American principle is destined to make its resounding progress round the world, not subjecting the nations to the yoke of a stranger, but annexing them to the principle of freedom, and of the combined administration of common interests, with absolute sovereignty in point of internal affairs, like the unprescribed juxtaposition of her silver stars on the common azure of her standard; it is not the principle of dominion which sits upon the banner of stars, but that of the self-government and absolute sovereignty of the individual; not the introduction of government but the abrogation of power and authority in the received acceptation of the word, is the gift which it is destined to cast into the lap of the nations.

Man's humanity is uniform; society is an indivisible whole; that which regulates society, the state, must needs share this universal unity. The World Republic, emanating from America, with America for standard-bearer, is the word which will hurl the dark sphinx of our time into her native abyss.

May this idea of the mission of America wake, in the old world, those reverberating echoes which, uniting with our voices, may rouse the instinctive, but as yet dormant, consciousness of the American people; may it be our fortune to produce the conviction of the unavoidable necessity of this task, which must lead a great people, conscious of its destiny, to inevitable triumph.

Disseminate the idea of American annexation among the drooping nations of Europe, cheer their hearts by clearly showing that in the mission of America is the assurance of their liberation,—and the undefined longing for the West, the despairing protest of emigration from the home of their birth, will give place to active exertions in removing the impediments which yet obstruct the fulfilment of this humanitary destiny,—"THE WORLD'S REPUBLIC, AS INITIATED BY AMERICA."

Opposed to the great questions of the highest material and moral interests of the race, and for which the Universal Republic affords the only practicable solution, the remnants of ancient culture, and the trammels of privileged classes, assume the form of paltry rubbish, which must soon, like chaff before the wind, give way before the charge of a youthful people, rushing forward irresistibly in the course of its fate.

Prepare the nations of Europe for the opening of the mighty coming drama in which America is destined to take the heroic part, of the historical advancement of the race. She is the land of promise, the land of the future, her future involves the destiny of the world.

It is for you to accelerate the work of history, and you will do so, mindful of the conviction more or less clearly expressed by the greatest men of Europe, that THE LIBERATION OF EUROPE IS THE FULFILMENT OF AMERICAN DESTINY.

APPENDIX H.

Report of the Committee on Military Organizations.

The League does not propose to enlist troops to serve against a foreign power, not declaredly at war with the United States Government.

There are in our midst a great number of exiles from the shores of Europe, anxious, at the first call of the trumpet, to return to the battles of freedom, and many American republicans determined to follow their example. To make their services effective it is important to procure them the nearest possible approach to a military education. We have in the 'Turners' League,' of this country, an organization, the design and purposes of which include this effort.

A number of the delegates of this Congress are also delegates at the Congress of Turners, to be held at Cincinnati. They are hereby commissioned to present the request of this Congress to take upon themselves the execution of the task, with such reference to the laws of various states facilitating the formation of militia and volunteer campanies, to the importance of a regard to the higher branches of a military institution, and to the powers to be vested in a central board, as the circumstances of place and time and their own judgment, may dictate.

APPENDIX I.

Report of the Committee on National Loans.

1. In regard to the German National Loan:

Preliminaries have been negotiated between the agent of the League, AMANDUS GOEGG, and the originator of the Loan, GOTTFRIED KINKEL, for the consolidation of the two organizations, based on the administration of the proceeds by the League, in consideration of their guaranteeing its validity. The articles were subjected to the ratification of the League on one part, and of the present guarantors and loan committees on the other. This has been declined by one-half of the latter, and thirteen of the former. It cannot therefore be entertained by the present Congress.

There is every reason in point of form to impede a consolidation, and none in point of substance, why the two undertakings should not subsist and prosper side by side, mutually aiding, but not interfering with each other. We therefore recommend this course of action.

But we hail the proposal as indicative of the virtual union in point of principle, already subsisting between the two undertakings, which we cordially recognize.

2. *In regard to the Hungarian National Loan.*

Whereas, Louis Kossuth, in his instructions to the German Committee of the National Loan resident at Philadelphia, and also in his letter to the Congress of the Revolutionary League, has declared that he looks upon the revolution necessary for the liberation of Hungary as equally necessary for the liberation of Germany, and that it is his intention to apply a portion of the funds to be collected by means of that loan to the latter purpose, which he justly considers identical with the former:

Whereas: that patriot has expressed a wish that the People's League should assist in bringing about the greatest possible circulation of the Hungarian bonds as a means to attain our common purpose:

Whereas: the solidarity of the peoples is a recognized fact, and threefore this Congress looks upon the furtherance of the National loan as of the highest importance; especially as that undertaking already enjoys the confidence of the greater portion of the American people, and has proved by far the most effective of all the means hitherto employed for the collection of material aid;

For these reasons, Congress resolves as follows:—

1. In consideration of the written declaration of L. Kossuth, that it is his intention to devote the funds obtained by the Hungarian loan in part to the revolutionary agitation of Germany, which he justly regards as identical with the success of the Hungarian Revolution—this Congress most earnestly recommends to the members of the League to facilitate the emission of the Hungarian bonds with their credit, their means, and their exertions.

2. That it is the particular request of Congress to the branch Unions of the League, that they will act as agents for the sale of the bonds, and for this purpose to communicate with the Kossuth Committee at Philadelphia.

The Congress of the People's League of the Old and New World, to the American People.

Hear us once more. You have listened to the appeals of bleeding Europe, poured forth in tones such as the world will never hear again. We do not offer to reiterate those efforts; what they could not accomplish is, upon that field, beyond the sphere of human powers.

They have not succeeded as we had hoped. The fact is too

clear for us to be unperceived, and we disdain to shrink from its avowal. But with men in whom a purpose has become absorbing, one failure is but a harvest of experience for future efforts. We have searched the causes of defeat, to make them means of victory; and we have found them.

Your sympathies were chilled at the outset by want of a uniform, settled, and tangible purpose, in the action of the European republicans with whom you were asked to co-operate. The hopeless confusion of jarring interests, the din of discordant traditions, and the clang of warring theories, presented a contrast to the calm, starry revolutions of your political system, which could not but repel you.

There was another obstacle, for which we have been disposed to blame you; unjustly, as more mature reflection has convinced us. The "pursuit of happiness" is recognized as the legitimate purpose of an American. Wealth is the material element of happiness; and the American pursues wealth as such. The proofs are abundant that he is ever ready to apply that wealth to the attainment of the worthier objects of life, and the welfare of his species; but the objects so favored must be those legitimately within the sphere of his purposes, those which, interwoven and combined, form a unity of his aims and objects. In his giving and his taking, his unity of purpose is never forgotten. Political purposes, above all others, are the recipients of your endowments; but to be so, they must fall within the sphere of your political sympathies; *and the political sympathies of America, are confined to the mission of the American Republic.*

If we have been disposed to make this a cause of complaint, we have done you wrong. We could not rightfully ask you to transfer your sympathies to the far distant steppes of the Theiss and the Danube, so long as we had not reared the bridge on which the American mind could easily traverse the void between. Your destiny is vast enough, and comprehensive enough for the energies of any people. We do not require you to go beyond it.—But we do ask as we are entitled to ask, that you should embrace your whole mission, and fulfil it.

What is the mission of the American Union?

In the year 1787 thirteen free States upon this continent found themselves suffering for want of a common commercial legislation, a united post office, equal coins, weights and measures, a uniform copy-right and patent law, security against a national bankruptcy, an irrevocable alliance for peace and war, the abolition of hereditary offices and standing armies, the extradition of criminals, the mutual recognition of matters of record, and a mutual guarantee of republican institutions. It was then that Alexander Hamilton told them that it was left for the people of these States to decide whether governments were destined forever to be the result of force and accident, or whether men were capable of forming States upon reflection and choice.

They executed the task; and at the head of their labors they inscribed the motto "E pluribus unum." They saw that as the ends of government are common to humanity, so should there be a unity of government among men to obtain these ends; they saw that a multiplicity of states dividing society, which is a single whole, is the result of imperfect civilization, and that it is the task of rational progress to displace it by a unity of the state.

Under this motto the American Union has advanced, unconsciously at times, but ever irresistibly. In the acquision of Louisiana the father of our independence was compelled to set his seal upon it. Texas and California followed the same inevitable bent. Cuba and Canada are conscious of the impending necessity. In Mexico we observe the formation of an ecclesiastical party desirous of annexation to the Holy Alliance, and a secular organization, eager to obtain admission into the American Union. Even the Islands of the Pacific, in the awakening dawn of their political life, manifest the same attractions. "The continent is ours," is fast becoming a recognized principle of our policy.

But what has a principle to do with continents? Principles are universal.

America is now more intricately connected with the European world, than were, at the time of the formation of the Union, the American States among themselves. The lightning is not yet the connecting medium of thought; but already the number of letters forwarded between the divided worlds has become incredible. Postal arrangements have scarcely time to be ratified, before new ones are necessary. The commercial relations are becoming more and more complicated, the rival products are driving each other from the market. The clashing laws of copyright and patents are becoming more and more unjust in their operation, the impunity of criminals is growing more flagrant and more dangerous from day to day. The emigration of a few short years is equal to the population of all the States that formed the Union. Every laboring family in Germanic Europe is represented in America.

All the classes of Europe that suffer from the past and present have set their hopes of the future on America.

Kossuth was their great plenipotentiary.

It is becoming daily more apparent, that the monarchs, having learned to look upon trade as a conductor of ideas, are resolved to close the territory they encumber against American trade. The internal commerce of America exceeds the external by a proportion which hardly leaves to the latter a figure in the scale. Yet the European states are inhabited by a people infinitely more numerous, more scantily supplied, and equally willing, if able, to return labor for merchandize, with any on the Western continent. The whole enormous difference is a tax upon our industry, to which America submits without representation.

The political misfortunes of Europe exert a continual influence upon her commercial situation; her commercial situation reacts upon ours.

Our Brokers are able to measure the percentage of European Oppression, and of American subjection.

American prosperity demands the disenthralment of European trade; American liberty requires the liberation of our European brethren; the American Union demands its extension over the States of Europe. The time has come for the strange device, "*E Pluribus Unum,*" to cross the Atlantic.

We call for the spread of American liberty. It may succeed without the cost of American blood or treasure. But thanks to the God of battles, it is more likely, that as Greece had her Trojan war, which transformed her from a fishing coast into the light of civilization, as the Crusades of Western Europe woke her from the night of ages, so America will have her Iliad and her crusade to achieve her place among the nations, as the focus of humanity. A war for the spread of our institutions is not a war of conquest; for, as the spirit of government is the principle of self-government, or rather, of non-government, its extension involves not the introduction, but the abrogation of force and violence; its purpose is to restore the sovereignity of the individual by removing the shackles against which he is vainly struggling.

The American continent divides the ocean, as Italy the Mediterranean; and as Rome of old looked forth upon the circle of lands that skirted that inland sea, so the United States of the modern world cast their eyes around upon the shores of Ocean. The universal Empire of the future, is her portion. The Empire, not of conquest and subjection, not of tradition and death, not of national rivalry and clannish hate, but of fraternity, equality and freedom. We invoke her to work out her destiny, and make One World of Many.

Wheeling, Va., Sept. 21, 1852.

www.ingramcontent.com/pod-product-compliance
Lightning Source LLC
LaVergne TN
LVHW011144110826
845150LV00008B/2504

9781418192020